by Iain Gray

WRITING *to* REMEMBER

WRITING *to* REMEMBER

79 Main Street, Newtongrange,
Midlothian EH22 4NA
Tel: 0131 344 0414   Fax: 0845 075 6085
E-mail: info@lang-syne.co.uk
www.langsyneshop.co.uk

Design by Dorothy Meikle
Printed by Printwell Ltd
© Lang Syne Publishers Ltd 2017

All rights reserved. No part of this publication may be reproduced, stored
or introduced into a retrieval system, or transmitted in any form or by any
means (electronic, mechanical, photocopying, recording or otherwise) without
the prior written permission of Lang Syne Publishers Ltd.

ISBN 978-1-85217-367-8

Gibson

MOTTO:
Open ye heavenly gates
(and)
Just and faithful.

CREST:
A pelican with blood
dripping from its chest.

TERRITORIES:
Galloway and eastern
shore of Loch Lomond.

NAME variations include:
Gib	Gibsoun
Gibb	Gilson
Gibbons	Gipson
Gibbsone	Gippson
Gibsons	

*Echoes of a far distant past
can still be found in most names*

Chapter one:

Origins of Scottish surnames

by George Forbes

It all began with the Normans.

For it was they who introduced surnames into common usage more than a thousand years ago, initially based on the title of their estates, local villages and chateaux in France to distinguish and identify these landholdings, usually acquired at the point of a bloodstained sword.

Such grand descriptions also helped enhance the prestige of these arrogant warlords and generally glorify their lofty positions high above the humble serfs slaving away below in the pecking order who only had single names, often with Biblical connotations as in Pierre and Jacques.

The only descriptive distinctions among this peasantry concerned their occupations, like Pierre the swineherd or Jacques the ferryman.

The Normans themselves were originally Vikings (or Northmen) who raided, colonised and eventually settled down around the French coastline.

They had sailed up the Seine in their longboats in 900 AD under their ferocious leader Rollo and ruled the roost in north east France before sailing over to conquer England, bringing their relatively new tradition of having surnames with them.

It took another hundred years for the Normans to percolate northwards and surnames did not begin to appear in Scotland until the thirteenth century.

These adventurous knights brought an aura of chivalry with them and it was said no damsel of any distinction would marry a man unless he had at least two names.

The family names included that of Scotland's great hero Robert De Brus and his compatriots were warriors from families like the De Morevils, De Umphravils, De Berkelais, De Quincis, De Viponts and De Vaux.

As the knights settled the boundaries of their vast estates, they took territorial names, as in Hamilton, Moray, Crawford, Cunningham, Dunbar, Ross, Wemyss, Dundas, Galloway, Renfrew, Greenhill, Hazelwood, Sandylands and Church-hill.

Other names, though not with any obvious geographical or topographical features, nevertheless derived from ancient parishes like Douglas, Forbes, Dalyell and Guthrie.

Other surnames were coined in connection with occupations, castles or legendary deeds. Stuart originated in the word steward, a prestigious post which was an integral part of any large medieval household. The same applied to Cooks, Chamberlains, Constables and Porters.

Borders towns and forts – needed in areas like the Debateable Lands which were constantly fought over by feuding local families – had their own distinctive names; and it was often from them that the resident groups took their communal titles, as in the Grahams of Annandale, the Elliots and Armstrongs of the East Marches, the Scotts and Kerrs of Teviotdale and Eskdale.

Even physical attributes crept into surnames, as in Small, Little and More (the latter being 'beg' in Gaelic), Long or Lang, Stark, Stout, Strong or Strang and even Jolly.

Mieklejohns would have had the strength of several men, while Littlejohn was named after the legendary sidekick of Robin Hood.

Colours got into the act with Black, White, Grey, Brown and Green (Red developed into Reid,

Ruddy or Ruddiman). Blue was rare and nobody ever wanted to be associated with yellow.

Pompous worthies took the name Wiseman, Goodman and Goodall.

Words intimating the sons of leading figures were soon affiliated into the language as in Johnson, Adamson, Richardson and Thomson, while the Norman equivalent of Fitz (from the French-Latin 'filius' meaning 'son') cropped up in Fitzmaurice and Fitzgerald.

The prefix 'Mac' was 'son of' in Gaelic and clans often originated with occupations – as in MacNab being sons of the Abbot, MacPherson and MacVicar being sons of the minister and MacIntosh being sons of the chief.

The church's influence could be found in the names Kirk, Clerk, Clarke, Bishop, Friar and Monk. Proctor came from a church official, Singer and Sangster from choristers, Gilchrist and Gillies from Christ's servant, Mitchell, Gilmory and Gilmour from servants of St Michael and Mary, Malcolm from a servant of Columba and Gillespie from a bishop's servant.

The rudimentary medical profession was represented by Barber (a trade which also once included dentistry and surgery) as well as Leech or Leitch.

Businessmen produced Merchants, Mercers, Monypennies, Chapmans, Sellers and Scales, while down at the old village watermill the names that cropped up included Miller, Walker and Fuller.

Other self explanatory trades included Coopers, Brands, Barkers, Tanners, Skinners, Brewsters and Brewers, Tailors, Saddlers, Wrights, Cartwrights, Smiths, Harpers, Joiners, Sawyers, Masons and Plumbers.

Even the scenery was utilised as in Craig, Moor, Hill, Glen, Wood and Forrest.

Rank, whether high or low, took its place with Laird, Barron, Knight, Tennant, Farmer, Husband, Granger, Grieve, Shepherd, Shearer and Fletcher.

The hunt and the chase supplied Hunter, Falconer, Fowler, Fox, Forrester, Archer and Spearman.

The renowned medieval historian Froissart, who eulogised about the romantic deeds of chivalry (and who condemned Scotland as being a poverty stricken wasteland), once sniffily dismissed the peasantry of his native France as the jacquerie (or the jacques-without-names) but it was these same humble folk who ended up overthrowing the arrogant aristocracy.

In the olden days, only the blueblooded knights of antiquity were entitled to full, proper names, both Christian and surnames, but with the passing of time and a more egalitarian, less feudal atmosphere, more respectful and worthy titles spread throughout the populace as a whole.

Echoes of a far distant past can still be found in most names and they can be borne with pride in commemoration of past generations who fought and toiled in some capacity or other to make our nation what it now is, for good or ill.

Chapter two:

For freedom's cause

Derived from 'Gib' or 'Gibb', shortened forms of the popular Middle Ages personal name 'Gilbert', the Gibson surname, indicating 'son of Gib/Gibb' has been present in Scotland from earliest times, originally in the form of 'Gibsoun.'

In England, in the form of 'Giselbert', it was popularised by those Normans who settled there in the wake of the Conquest of 1066 and, in common with many other Anglo-Norman families, bearers of the Giselbert/Gilbert name settled in Scotland in the twelfth century.

But evidence that bearers of the Gibsoun/Gibson name were here for a considerable period before comes from the fact that there is a record of a Gibsoun of Rothesay, on the Isle of Bute, in the ninth century.

This fuses with evidence that the original territory of the Gibsouns/Gibsons was Galloway, in the southwest of Scotland, and that they may have descended from Irish tribes who first settled there and at other locations on Scotland's western seaboard, particularly Argyll, from about 500 A.D.

Indeed the early history of bearers of the name, in all its variants of spelling, concerns those who were settled on the western seaboard.

Along with clans that include those of Dewar, Hammond, MacAusland, MacCormack, Morris, Ruskin, Watson, Weir and Yuill, the Gibsons are recognised as a sept, or sub-branch, of Clan Buchanan.

This ancient clan, who trace a descent from Anselan O'Kyan, the son of an Ulster chieftain, have the motto of 'Brighter hence the honour' and crest of a hand holding a crown.

The O'Kyans took the Buchanan name from the lands of Buchanan, on the eastern shore of Loch Lomond, around Killearn, which were granted to them in the early years of the thirteenth century.

One possible explanation of the Gibson-Buchanan link is that, bearing in mind 'Gibson' originally derives from 'Gilbert', the original grant of the Buchanan lands was to a *Gilbert* O'Kyan.

It is not known if those Gibsons settled in Galloway were of a different branch from those settled in close kinship with the Buchanans of Loch Lomond.

But what is known with certainty is that both the Galloway and the Loch Lomond Gibsons, along with Clan Buchanan, were staunchly allied to the cause of the great warrior king Robert the Bruce during Scotland's bitter and bloody Wars of Independence.

A Johun Gibson, keeper of the strategically important Rothesay Castle, is known to have turned the keys of the fortress over to Bruce during his bold campaign to evict the English garrisons that had been stationed throughout Scotland by England's Edward I, known and feared as 'the Hammer of the Scots.'

It is also known that Clan Buchanan and their kinsfolk such as the Gibsons fought for the cause of Scotland's independence at the battle of Bannockburn of June 1314. This was when a 20,000-strong English army under Edward I's successor, Edward II, was defeated by a Scots army less than half this strength.

By midsummer of 1313 the mighty fortress of Stirling Castle was occupied by an English garrison under the command of Sir Philip Mowbray, and Bruce's brother, Edward, agreed to a pledge by Mowbray that if the castle was not relieved by battle by midsummer of the following year, then he would surrender.

This made battle inevitable, and by June 23 of 1314 the two armies faced one another at Bannockburn, in sight of the castle.

It was on this day that Bruce slew the English knight Sir Henry de Bohun in single combat, but the battle proper was not fought until the following day, shortly after the rise of the midsummer sun.

The English cavalry launched a desperate but futile charge on the densely packed ranks of Scottish spearmen known as schiltrons, and by the time the sun had sank slowly in the west the English army had been totally routed.

Scotland's independence had been secured, to the glory of Bruce and his loyal supporters such as the Gibsons, and at terrible cost to the English.

But Gibsons also frequently tasted the bitter fruits of defeat at the hands of their southern neighbour, most memorably at the battle of Flodden, when a contingent of Gibsons and Patrick Buchanan, the eldest son of the Buchanan Chief, were among the 5,000 Scots killed. The Scottish death toll also included James IV, an archbishop, two bishops, eleven earls, fifteen barons and 300 knights.

The Scottish monarch had embarked on the venture after Queen Anne of France, under the terms of the Auld Alliance between Scotland and her nation, appealed to him to 'break a lance' on her behalf and act as her chosen knight.

Crossing the border into England at the head of a 25,000-strong army that included 7,500 clansmen and their kinsmen, James engaged a 20,000-strong force commanded by the Earl of Surrey.

But, despite their numerical superiority and bravery, the Scots proved no match for the skilled English artillery and superior military tactics of Surrey, and those not slaughtered on the field of battle were forced to flee in confusion.

In a later and even bloodier conflict, Gibsons and the Chief of Clan Buchanan were among the 14,000 Scots killed at the battle of Pinkie.

Fought on September 10, 1547, near Musselburgh, in East Lothian, a 25,000-strong English army under the Duke of Somerset decisively defeated a 35,000-strong Scots army under the Earl of Arran.

The battle had been fought during the 'Rough Wooing', an attempt by England's dynastically ambitious Henry VIII to force upon the Scots agreement for the future marriage of his infant son Edward to the infant Mary, Queen of Scots.

Despite their superior numbers, what led to the defeat of the Scots was that Somerset was backed by a fleet of naval guns at the mouth of the River Esk, and the early loss in the battle of the Scots cavalry after it launched a premature and wild charge on the massed and disciplined English ranks.

Gibsons, under the banner of the Chief of Clan Buchanan, also fought and died for the Royalist cause during the civil war that ravaged Scotland between 1638 and 1649.

This was a brutal struggle between those Presbyterian Scots who had signed a National Covenant that opposed the divine right of the Stuart monarchy and Royalists such as James Graham, 1st Marquis of Montrose, whose prime allegiance was to Charles I.

Although Montrose had initially supported the Covenant, his conscience later forced him to switch sides and, allied with clans such as the Buchanans and their Gibson kinsfolk, he embarked on a series of campaigns from 1644 to 1645 – a year that became known as the Year of Miracles because of his brilliant military successes.

At the Battle of Inverlochy, on February 2, 1645, the Earl of Argyll was forced to flee after 1,500 of his troops were wiped out in a surprise attack.

Montrose enjoyed another great victory at the battle of Kilsyth in August, but final and decisive defeat came less than a month later at Philiphaugh, near Selkirk.

Chapter three:

Kidnapping and commerce

Away from the blood and gore of the battlefield, other bearers of the Gibson name accrued lands and powerful positions.

A Thome Gibson is recorded in the 15th century as holding lands in the area of the town of Dumfries, while in the early years of the sixteenth century a notable family of the name acquired estates in Fife.

These were the Gibsons of Durie, one of whom, Alexander Gibson of Durie, fell victim in the early years of the seventeenth century to the state of near anarchy that then prevailed in Scotland.

The frightening scale of this lawlessness and disregard for human life that then blighted the land from the Borders to the Highlands and Islands, can be found in a shocking report submitted to the Scottish Parliament in 1616 by Sir Thomas Hamilton, the Lord Binning.

Edinburgh, he wrote in graphic terms, was

'the ordinary place of butchery, revenge and daily fights; the parish churches and churchyards being more frequented upon the Sunday for advantages of neighbourly malice and mischief, nor for God's service.

'Noblemen, barons, gentlemen and people of all sorts being slaughtered as it were in public and uncontrollable hostilities.'

Merchants and civic officials going about their daily business were constantly in danger of their lives, Lord Binning fumed, stating how they were 'robbed and left for dead in daylight, going to their markets and fairs of Montrose, Wigtown and Berwick.

'Ministers being dirked in Stirling, buried quick in Liddesdale, and murdered in Galloway. Merchants of Edinburgh being waited in their passage to Leith to be made prisoners and ransomed.'

It was the fate of Alexander Gibson of Durie during these lawless times to be seized, bound, gagged and kidnapped by a heavily armed band of Borderers while strolling one day along the sea beach near his home.

Carried over the Forth to Leith, then to Edinburgh and through Melrose to the Borders, he was then taken into England and confined for a time in Harbottle Castle.

At the time of his abduction, Gibson held the important but now defunct Scottish legal post of 'reporter of decisions', and had been kidnapped by a Borderer and his retainers in a bid for the Borderer to obtain a favourable verdict at a forthcoming court case involving the beneficiaries of a will.

For reasons that remain obscure, it was considered that the absence of Gibson in court would help the Borderer's case.

The outcome of the case is not known, but the hapless Gibson of Durie was eventually released from his grim confinement and went on to become a Lord of Session.

In the West of Scotland, the seventeenth century entrepreneur Walter Gibson is credited with having helped to lay the foundations of Glasgow's wealth.

Already the owner of a malt making business, in 1688 he launched a new business venture exporting herring from the Clyde to France, the vessels returning with valuable cargoes of brandy and salt.

The lucrative business made Gibson immensely wealthy, and in addition to owning fishing rights on Glasgow's River Kelvin, he owned coal seams in the district of Camlachie.

Laird of Glasgow districts that included

Govan, Bellahouston, Whiteinch and Hyndland, he was also the city's Lord Provost for a time.

But his business empire collapsed in the wake of the Darien Scheme, an ambitious but ultimately disastrous attempt to establish a Scottish merchant colony at Darien, across the Isthmus of Panama, in Central America.

Gibson was one of the many Scots investors who lost large sums of money in the enterprise and, imprisoned for a time for debt, he lost the bulk of his properties.

Another lucrative business venture in which he had been involved was the transportation from the Clyde to the colonies of those religious dissidents known as the Covenanters, aboard his vessel *Pelican*.

His downfall, many claimed at the time, was God's punishment for this.

Other entrepreneurs of the Gibson name have been rather more fortunate in their business ventures.

Born in 1819 near St Andrews, New Brunswick, Alexander Gibson was the Canadian industrialist better known by his nickname of "Boss" Gibson.

Owner of a sawmill and a forest in New Brunswick's Fredericton area, Gibson, who died in

1913, was also responsible for establishing no less than two railway lines – the New Brunswick Railway and the Canada Eastern Railway.

One particularly notable bearer of the Gibson name was Wing Commander Guy Gibson, of 'Dambusters' fame and a recipient of the Victoria Cross, the highest award for bravery for British and Commonwealth forces.

Born in 1918 in Simla, India, he was awarded the Distinguished Flying Cross in July of 1940 for his exploits as a bomber pilot, while in 1943 he was selected to command 617 Squadron, tasked with the destruction of dams in the Ruhr area of Nazi Germany.

The operation, utilising 19 Lancaster bombers loaded with the 'bouncing bombs' developed by the scientist Barnes Wallis, was carried out on the evening of May 16, 1943, and resulted in the destruction of the Moehne and Edur dams and the subsequent heavy flooding of a large part of the Ruhr.

Only eleven bombers, including that of Gibson and his crew, survived the raid, and it was because of the valour he displayed on the mission and on previous missions, that he was awarded the Victoria Cross.

In September of 1944, Gibson and his navigator were killed when their de Havilland Mosquito crashed near Steenbergen, in the Netherlands.

Before his death, Gibson, who was also a recipient of America's Legion of Merit, wrote his autobiographical *Enemy Coast Ahead*.

Two titled and rather eccentric bearers of the Gibson name were the Honourable Violet Gibson and her brother William, 2nd Baron Ashbourne.

Their father was Edward Gibson, 1st Baron Ashbourne, the Irish lawyer born in Dublin in 1837 who went on to become a Lord Chancellor of Ireland.

The eminently respectable 1st Baron's daughter, Violet, gained international notoriety when, in April of 1926, and for reasons known only to herself, she attempted to assassinate the Italian fascist dictator Benito Mussolini in Rome.

The Honourable Violet shot the dictator as he sat in a car – but despite being shot three times, twice in the nose, he remarkably survived relatively unscathed.

Violet narrowly escaped being lynched by a furious mob, and it was only thanks to Mussolini's personal intervention that, thought to be mentally ill, she was deported back to Britain, She died in an asylum in 1956.

Her older brother William Gibson, 2nd Baron Ashbourne, born in Dublin in 1868 and who died in 1942, shocked the Establishment of his day by espousing the cause of native Irish culture, converting from the Protestant faith to Catholicism, adopting traditional Irish dress and speaking only Irish in the House of Lords.

This proved too much for his relations, who successfully arranged for the bulk of the family estate to be passed to a younger brother, Edward, who succeeded as the 3rd Baron Ashbourne.

Chapter four:

On the world stage

Bearers of the Gibson name achieved fame at an international level, not least in the world of film.

Born in 1956 in Peekskill, New York, **Mel Gibson** is the acclaimed actor, producer, director and screenwriter who left the USA for Australia with his family when aged 12.

Educated at St Leo's Catholic College in Wahroonga, New South Wales, he went on to learn the basics of the acting craft at Sydney's Institute of Dramatic Art, where he appeared in a number of stage plays.

His performance as a mentally-challenged youth in the 1979 *Tim* led to an Australian Film Institute Award for Best Actor in a Leading Role, with his first major film role coming in the same year when he starred in the first of the *Mad Max* movies.

Further film roles include the 1981 *Gallipoli* and, in 1982, *The Year of Living Dangerously*.

Other major film and directing roles include the *Lethal Weapon* series, the 1990 *Air America*, the 1995 *Braveheart* and the 2003 *The Passion of Christ*, for which he also wrote the screenplay.

Honoured as an Officer of the Order of Australia in recognition of his service's to the nation's film industry, he is a son of **Hutton "Red" Gibson**, the controversial proponent of what is known as Traditional Catholicism, and who was born in New York in 1918.

An advocate of a number of conspiracy theories, he is also the author of the 1983 *Time Out of Mind* and the 2003 *The Enemy is Still Here!*

Back to the stage, **Tyrese Gibson**, born in 1978 in Watts, Los Angeles is the American actress and singer whose film roles include the 2004 *Flight of the Phoenix* and the 2007 *Transformers*, while **Brian Gibson** was the English film director who was born in Reading in 1944.

Beginning as a research assistant for the BBC, he went on to produce a number of editions of the science series *Horizon*, receiving a 1975 BAFTA Award and the Prix Italia Award for the *Horizon* production *Joey*, concerning a brain-damaged child.

Gibson, who died in 2004, also produced a number of films that include the 1980 *Breaking Glass*, the 1986 *Poltergeist II: The Other Side* and the 1993 bio-pic on singer Tina Turner, *Tina (What's Love Got to Do with It)*.

Born in 1935 in Germantown, Pennsylvania, James Bateman was the American actor and songwriter who chose the stage name of **Henry Gibson**, as a play on the name of the Norwegian dramatist Henrik Ibsen.

His first role was in the 1963 Jerry Lewis film *The Nutty Professor*, but he is best remembered as one of the regular cast members of the American television comedy *Rowan and Martin's Laugh-In*, and for his role from 2004 to 2005 in the television drama *Boston Legal*.

Other film roles include the 1980 *The Blues Brothers* and the 2008 *Big Stan*, while he also wrote the title music for the 1975 *Nashville*; he died in 2009.

Born in 1892 in Tekamah, Nebraska, Edmund Richard Gibson was the American film actor, director, producer and rodeo champion better known as **Hoot Gibson**.

Learning to ride a horse when only a young lad, he later became a star attraction at rodeos throughout North America, winning the steer roping championship at the 1912 Calgary Stampede.

His riding skills brought him to the attention of cowboy movie producers, and he subsequently appeared in a number of films that include *Pride of the Range* and *His Only Son*.

Inducted into the Western Performers Hall of Fame at the National Cowboy and Western Heritage Museum in Oklahoma City, Gibson, who died in 1962, also has a star on the Hollywood Walk of Fame.

Bearers of the Gibson name have also excelled, and continue to excel, in the highly competitive world of sport.

The first African-American to compete on the World Tennis Tour and the first to win a Grand Slam title, **Althea Gibson** was the top female tennis player who was born into a poor background in Silver, South Carolina, in 1927.

Her family later moved to Harlem, in New York, where she joined a local tennis club – this at a time when competition in the sport was racially segregated.

It was not until an editorial denouncing segregation in the sport appeared in an issue of American Lawn Tennis magazine that she was allowed to participate in the 1950 U.S. Championships, breaking the colour barrier for the first time.

Winner of the 1955 Italian Championship, she went on the following year to win the first of several Grand Slam titles of her career.

These wins included two consecutive

Wimbledon singles championships and three consecutive Women's Doubles titles in the 1950s and the 1957 U.S. Championship.

The tennis star, who died in 2003, was inducted into the U.S. Open Court of Champions in 2007 and, two years later, the New Jersey Hall of Fame.

In baseball, **Bob Gibson**, born in 1935 in Omaha, Nebraska, is the former pitcher who, after playing for a time in the 1950s with the famed Harlem Globetrotters, later played for the St Louis Cardinals.

Elected to the Baseball Hall of Fame in 1981, he also has a star on the St Louis Walk of Fame.

Also a member of the Baseball Hall of Fame, **Joshua Gibson**, born in 1911 in Buena Vista, Georgia, and who died in 1947, was the catcher who played in the former Negro Leagues – at a time when African-Americans were barred from playing in Major League.

In the fast-paced game of ice hockey, **Billy Gibson**, born in Lethbridge in 1927 and who died in 2006, was the Canadian player who helped his national team win a gold medal at the 1952 Winter Olympics.

In the creative world of music, **Sir Alexander Gibson** was the internationally acclaimed Scottish conductor who was born in 1926 in Motherwell, Lanarkshire.

His musical studies commenced at the Royal Scottish Academy of Music and Drama (RSAMD) in Glasgow, and by the age of only 34 he was appointed musical director at Sadler's Wells Opera.

A number of other prestigious posts followed, including his appointment in 1959 as the first Scottish principal conductor and artistic director of the Royal National Orchestra and principal conductor of the equally prestigious Houston Symphony Orchestra.

Knighted for his services to music in 1977, he died in 1995, and is commemorated by a bust in Glasgow's Theatre Royal, now the home of Scottish Opera, while the Alexander Gibson School of Opera, part of the RSAMD, is named in his honour.

In a different musical genre, **Bob Gibson** was the American folk singer, banjo and twelve-string guitar player who was born in Brooklyn, New York, in 1931.

Credited with having led the folk music revival of the late 1950s and early 1960s, albums he recorded before his death in 1996 include *Offbeat Folksongs*, *There's A Meetin' Here Tonight* and the 1980 *The Perfect High*.

Best known for his work on the late 1990s' Broadway musical revivals of *Cabaret* and *Steel Pier* and his creative work on the 1978 movie *Grease*, **Michael Gibson** was the American musician and orchestrator who was born in 1944 and died in 2005.

Born in Los Angeles in 1942, **Jill Gibson** is the American singer, songwriter and artist who is best known for having been a member for a brief period in 1964 of the band The Mamas and the Papas, while **Debbie Gibson**, born in New York in 1970, has the distinction of having been, at the age of 17, the youngest artiste ever to write, produce and perform a U.S. Number One single, with her song *Foolish Beat*.

In the realms of country music, **Don Gibson**, born in 1928 in Shelby, North Carolina was the musician and songwriter who wrote such enduring country hits as *I Can't Stop Loving You* and *Oh Lonesome Me*.

Inducted into the Nashville Songwriters Hall of Fame in 1973 and the Country Music Hall of Fame in 2001, he died in 2003.

One bearer of the Gibson name who was responsible for a particularly notable contribution to the world of music was the instrument maker **Orville H. Gibson**, born in 1856 in Chateaugay, New York, and who died in 1918.

It was from his workshops in Kalamazoo,

Michigan, that he crafted a distinctive style of guitar – laying the foundations of the famed Gibson Guitar Corporation of today.

In the world of art, **Aubrey Gibson**, born in 1901 in Kew, Melbourne, and who died in 1973, was the Australian businessman, art collector and patron of the arts who was a founding director in the early 1950s of both the Elizabethan Theatre Trust and the National Trust of Australia.

In literature, **Wilfred Gibson**, born in 1878 in Hexham, Northumberland was the British poet of the First World War who is among sixteen poets of the conflict who is commemorated on a slate in Westminster Abbey's Poets Corner.

The poet, famous for his war poem *Breakfast and Back*, also wrote a number of works unrelated to the war, including *Flannan Isle*; he died in 1962.

Born in 1914, **William Gibson** was the Tony Award-winning American novelist and playwright best known for his 1959 play *The Miracle Worker*; he died in 2008.

Responsible for coining the term 'cyberspace' and popularising it through his 1984 novel *Neuromancer*, **William Gibson**, born in 1948 in Conway, South Carolina, is the American-Canadian science fiction writer who specialises in the genre known as 'cyberpunk.'

In the field of graphic art, **Charles Dana Gibson** was the artist, born in 1867 in Roxbury Massachusetts, best known for his creation of the iconic *Gibson Girl*, representative of attractive and independent American women of the early years of the twentieth century.

A contributor to magazines that included *Life*, *Colliers* and *Harper's Weekly*, he eventually became the owner and editor of *Life* in 1918.

The Gibson Martini, garnished with a pickled onion rather than an olive or lemon zest, is named in his honour, while he was featured on the cover of *TIME* magazine in 1927; he died in 1944.

It is not only on the terrestrial level that bearers of the Gibson name have stamped their mark – but also in the realms of deepest outer space.

Born in 1936 in Buffalo, New York, **Edward Gibson** is a former astronaut with the American space agency NASA.

One of the crew of Skylab4, launched in 1973, he is the proud recipient of the NASA Distinguished Service Medal and a member of the US Astronaut Hall of Fame.